The Collegeville

Church History
TIME-LINE

JOSEPH F. KELLY

CONTENTS

Liturgical Press
Collegeville, Minnesota
www.litpress.org

1 2 3 4 5 6 7 8
Library of Congress Control Number: 2004114342

ISBN-13: 978-0-8146-2834-8
ISBN-10: 0-8146-2834-6

Worldwide co-edition produced by Lion Hudson plc, Mayfield House, 256 Banbury Road, Oxford OX2 7DH, England
Tel: +44 (0) 1865 302750
Fax +44 (0) 1865 302757
Email: coed@lionhudson.com
www.lionhudson.com

Designed by Peter Wyart

Maps
Hardlines, Oxford

Photographs
Tim Dowley: pp. 6, 13, 14, 15, 17, 19,
Empics: p. 24
Impact: p. 23
Illustrated London News: p. 21
Liturgical Press: pp. 2, 8, 20
Ann Ronan: p. 14
Peter Wyart: pp. 10 (top), 11, 12

Illustrations;
David Price: p. 15
Paul Wyart: p. 8

Joseph F. Kelly, Ph. D., is professor of religious studies and chair of that department at John Carroll University in Cleveland, Ohio. *The World of the Early Christians* (1997), *The Problem of Evil in the Western Tradition* (2002), *Responding to Evil* (2003), and *The Origins of Christmas* (2004), published by the Liturgical Press, are among his previous books.

Introduction

The Catholic church is the Body of Christ, and, under the inspiration and guidance of the Holy Spirit, it continues the work of Christ in the world. The Catholic church is also a human institution, composed of fallible people like us, striving to do what is right, failing, striving again, and always asking the Lord's help in our efforts. Inevitably, we, the People of God, have not always lived up to the Lord's calling. The church has produced those who lived lives of noble sanctity and those who lived lives of great disillusionment to their fellow Catholics. Sometimes members of this second group held high offices in the church, and while they will always disappoint us, they should not always surprise us. We should not overlook such people, but, on the other hand, we should always remember that the church is greater than the sum of its individual members. We should also always remember that even in the worst times, the church was graced with great saints and, perhaps more importantly, a lot of good Catholics who preserved the church's ideals in quiet but crucial ways.

Historians joke that in history the only constant is change, but many Catholics find difficulty with the notion that the church changes. The divine element, the presence of the Spirit, never changes, but human practices do. The Second Vatican Council (1962–1965) offers the best examples of this. For centuries Catholics prayed in Latin, a language few understood, but Vatican II urged people to pray in the vernacular. That may be all right, but surely doctrine does not change? Not in the sense that the church teaches one thing on one day and the exact opposite the next day. But doctrine does develop as the popes, bishops, theologians and people get deeper and fuller – and in those senses, newer – understandings of

St. Peter and St. Paul depicted on a medallion.

doctrine. Before the council, the church was often conceived in a hierarchical way, but Vatican II defined the church as the entire People of God. This new understanding did not do away with the hierarchical one but rather emphasized a broader approach, keeping the old but adding the new. This is important to remember because in this pilgrimage through church history we will encounter numerous examples of change.

A final point before we begin our journey. We routinely use the phrase "the Catholic church," but the correct title is "the Roman Catholic Church." The word "catholic" means universal, and it was used to differentiate the belief of the whole church from the views of dissident sects. In the Roman and medieval periods, the term "Christian" was usually used instead of "Roman Catholic" because the church often confronted people who did not follow Christ, such as pagans or Muslims, but this is the same church, regardless of the term. Since the Protestant Reformation, the term "Catholic church" has been the most common designation.

The Roman Catholic Church originated at Pentecost and has not just survived but flourished through 2,000 years as it strives to make Christ a presence in the world. The church has a remarkable history, so let us turn to it now.

The First Century

[Je]sus died somewhere between 30 [a]nd 33 A.D. (Latin for *Anno Domini*, [i]n the year of the Lord"). His [di]spirited disciples knew they had [to] continue his work, but they hesi[ta]ted to act decisively. The Holy [S]pirit descended upon them at [P]entecost, and under divine inspira[ti]on, the disciples began to preach [fe]arlessly in Jerusalem, making [m]any converts but also encounter[in]g opposition, as the martyrdom of [St]ephen showed. One of their [fi]ercest opponents was a man [n]amed Saul who went to Damascus [in] Syria, where some disciples had [e]vangelized. But Saul had a conver[si]on experience on the road to [D]amascus and became a fearless [p]reacher and apostle known as [Pa]ul.

[ ]The earliest disciples were Jewish [a]nd had preached only to Jews, but [so]me Gentiles had heard the mes[sa]ge and wished to become [C]hristian. The disciples accepted [th]em but did not know whether [G]entiles should have to follow the Jewish Law. Some disciples said yes, but Paul said no. After some soul-searching, the church leaders agreed with Paul, who then evangelized heavily in the Eastern Mediteranean area and even in Rome. He also produced the first Christian literature, his epistles, in which we find the first teachings about Jesus, the church, and the sacraments.

As Christianity spread, some people came to fear it as a revolutionary movement. Christians suffered opposition everywhere, and in the year 64 the emperor persecuted the Roman community, a persecution that took the life of Peter and possibly of Paul, who also died around the same time. Little is known of Peter's stay in Rome, but as the leader of the Twelve Apostles, he would also have led the local community and be a natural target for the persecutors. But no persecution immediately followed this one, and the church enjoyed some peace.

Around the year 70 the evangelist Mark wrote the first gospel, record-ing traditions about Jesus which had been passed on orally for decades. In the 80s Matthew and Luke followed him, as did John circa 100. These four documents form the basis of what later Christians would know about Jesus. Possibly the first three were written in or around Antioch, a port city in Syria where Jesus' disciples were first called Christians, that is, followers of the *Christos*, Greek for "the Anointed One" or "the Messiah."

For the rest of century several Greek writers, now anonymous, produced the additional literature, mostly pastoral, that would eventually make up the New Testament. These pseudo-Pauline letters and Catholic epistles show diverse communities experimenting with forms of organization as Christians learned to live in the world. Little is known about particular churches, although Rome and Antioch emerged as regional leaders, an important development as church leaders increasingly rejected the view found in the Apocalypse that the world would end soon. They believed that the church had a future on earth, and, as we know, they were right.

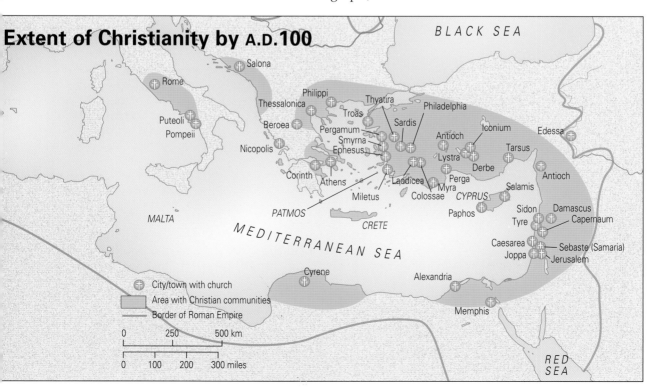

Extent of Christianity by A.D. 100

BLACK SEA

Salona · Rome · Puteoli · Pompeii · Nicopolis · Philippi · Thessalonica · Troas · Beroea · Pergamum · Smyrna · Ephesus · Corinth · Athens · Thyatira · Sardis · Philadelphia · Antioch · Iconium · Edessa · Tarsus · Lystra · Derbe · Laodicea · Perga · Myra · Colossae · CYPRUS · Antioch · Salamis · Paphos · Sidon · Tyre · Damascus · Capernaum · Caesarea · Joppa · Sebaste (Samaria) · Jerusalem · PATMOS · Miletus · MALTA · CRETE · MEDITERRANEAN SEA · Cyrene · Alexandria · Memphis · RED SEA

City/town with church
Area with Christian communities
Border of Roman Empire

0   250   500 km
0   100   200   300 miles

The Second Century

St. Polycarp, an early Christian martyr.

Christian communities were scattered around the Roman Empire in this century, although the majority of the faithful lived in the Greek-speaking areas of the Eastern Mediterranean (Greece, Syria, Asia Minor [=modern Turkey], and Egypt). In the Latinized West most lived in Italy, but as the century went on, Christian communities appeared in Britain, North Africa, and Gaul [=modern France]. As believers realized the world would not end soon, church leadership moved from charismatic figures to ministries better suited to continuity, such as deacons, priests, and bishops.

Christians suffered more persecutions in the second century, but these were sporadic and localized. Victims ranged from peasants to important bishops such as Polycarp of Smyrna in Asia Minor. Bits of evidence show that some Romans realized the growth of the church would threaten traditional Roman values, thus setting the stage for more persecutions. Yet educated Christians hoped that church and empire could co-exist, and we find several writers of this period using classical philosophy to explain aspects of Christian doctrine.

The main problem for the church in the second century was establishing the authorities to which Christians could turn to know what was right doctrine and practice. Some educated Greek converts believed that a spiritual deity would be contaminated by contact with flesh, and while they accepted that Jesus had a body, they thought it was not important since he saved the world not by his suffering and death but by bringing it knowledge – *gnosis* in Greek, which is why they were called Gnostics. They claimed that their teachings had been passed along secretly in Gnostic groups from the days of the apostles.

In the middle of the century a conservative reaction broke out when a man named Montanus claimed the Holy Spirit was speaking through him, and his prophecies obviated the need for sacred books or ecclesiastical organization. Where did Truth

St. Irenaeus, the great Gallic theologian.

reside – in the Gnostic secret traditions, in Montanist prophecies, or in the mainstream communities? A Gallic theologian named Irenaeus of Lyons had the answer.

Irenaeus created theological method. He pointed out that all Christian teaching derived from the apostles and that their teaching could be found in Scripture and Tradition, expanding the notion of Scripture to include the New Testament. He located tradition in the public teachings of bishops of sees founded by the apostles and used Rome as the chief example — no more secret traditions, no more wild prophecies, but the Word of God and ecclesiastical tradition that Irenaeus understood as something organic, reaching back to the apostles but with every generation contributing to it.

Anti-Christian graffiti scratched in a Roman wall. The boy is shown worshiping a crucified figure with a donkey's head.

The Third Century

In this century Christian intellectual life emerged on the south shore of the Mediterranean. In North Africa, the theologians Tertullian (*ca.* 160-*ca.* 20) and Cyprian (d. 258) composed the first important Latin theological treatises. Words like *sacramentum* (sacrament) and *Trinitas* (Trinity) made their first appearance in church history. But the North Africans had a very narrow view of the church, seeing it as a rigid community of the elect few; they also feared and rejected pagan culture.

In Alexandria in Egypt, the theologians Clement (d. *ca.* 215) and Origen (185–254) pioneered systematic theology, recognizing that our understanding of the church must harmonize with our understanding of Christ, which in turn should harmonize with our understanding of God. Origen also founded the science of biblical study or exegesis. The Alexandrian Christians took what was good in pagan culture,

and incorporated Greek philosophical elements into their theology. This would become a standard theological method, especially among the scholastic theologians of the High Middle Ages.

The theologians had difficulty with the notion of the Trinity, fearing that if they said Father and Son were both divine, this would compromise monotheism. Subordinationism, the belief that the Son was divine but inferior to the Father, became the most common view, even though theologians recognized its shortcomings.

The see of Rome emerges clearly in this century. Pope Callistus I (217–222) rejected the African concept of an elect community, recognizing that all humans are sinners and the church is the mother of all. Callistus also expanded the notion of penance so that Christians could receive it when they needed remission from their sins.

In 256 the Roman church disagreed with the Africans over whether Christian heretics needed to be baptized when received back into the church. Africa said yes, but Rome said a laying on of hands would suffice. In the debate, Pope Stephen I became the first pope to speak with the authority of St. Peter. The Africans were unmoved, but this understanding of the papacy would grow in importance over the coming centuries.

The Roman state began to persecute the Christians more frequently and in 250 launched the first empire-wide persecution, which ended with the emperor's accidental death. Tensions remained high for the rest of the century, but the persecutions faded out.

The third century also saw the first Christian art, mostly frescoes in the Roman catacombs and some statuary. Since the Jews did not make images, this shows the Christians had decided that this aspect of pagan culture did not conflict with their faith. Later generations of Christians owe this generation a great debt. Christianity without art seems almost inconceivable.

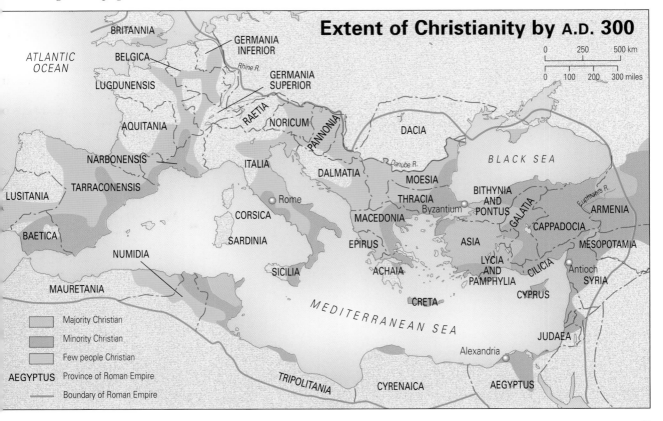

Extent of Christianity by A.D. 300

The Fourth Century

Except for the era of Jesus himself, the fourth century is the most significant period in church history. A Roman emperor, Constantine I (306–337), converted to Christianity, ending the persecutions and allowing the Christians to evangelize freely. They succeeded brilliantly, and by the end of the century the Roman Empire had become an officially Christian state. Under the patronage of the emperors and wealthy nobles, the Christians built magnificent churches, especially in Constantine's new city, Constantinople, on the Bosporus of what is now Turkey, and in Rome where Saint Peter's was one of several great basilicas. But the emperors considered themselves to be sacred persons, chosen by God to rule, and tension arose whenever church and state mixed, a tension that would grow in the Middle Ages.

An Egyptian priest named Arius denied the divinity of the Son in the Trinity, and, at the emperor's urging, the bishops of the inhabited world (*oikumene* in Greek) assembled at Nicaea in 325 for the first ecumenical council, which affirmed the equality and divinity of Father and Son. But the questions raised by Arius did not die out, and in 381 the second ecumenical council, Constantinople I, reaffirmed Nicaea's teaching and taught the equality and divinity of the Spirit as well. The council produced the creed we now know as the Nicene Creed and used Greco-Roman philosophical terminology, for example, the *persons* of the Trinity share in the one divine *substance*. The Christians had decided it was acceptable to use positive elements of Greco-Roman culture.

This was an age of great theologians, such as Athanasius, the hero of the Nicene cause, Ambrose of Milan, the biblical translator Jerome, and John Chrysostom, the great preacher. Theology achieved a status that would not be matched until the twelfth century.

This century also saw the formal recognition of the great bishoprics (Rome, Alexandria, Constantinople). In the East, Rome had a primacy of honor, but in the West it had a primacy of jurisdiction, as Rome became the unquestioned leader of the Latin Christians.

But the church's newfound prominence and grandeur disturbed some morally keen Christians, who retreated to the deserts of the East, founding monasticism, a dissident movement that would one day dominate Christian intellectual and spiritual life.

At the end of the century an ominous note sounded when the Germanic barbarians, kept at bay for so long, began to enter the empire, bringing political and religious problems.

Above: **Great sculpted head of Constantine.**

Left: **Mosaic of St. Ambrose of Milan, one of the great theologians of the age.**

Below: **St. Jerome, renowned for his Latin translation of the Bible, the Vulgate. This statue stands in Bethlehem, where Jerome lived towards the end of his life.**

The Fifth Century

St. Augustine of Hippo writing his celebrated book The City of God.

In the fifth century the dam burst. Germanic barbarians crossed the Rhine, moved into Spain, crossed the seas into Britain and North Africa, and in 410 captured Rome itself. In 476 the Roman Empire came to an end in Western Europe, ushering in the Middle Ages and presenting the church with the awesome problem of evangelizing the barbarians, most of whom were pagans.

But the Roman candle flickered brightly before going out. Beautiful new churches, such as Santa Sabina in Rome, continued to be built, and the greatest of all ancient Latin theologians, the North African Augustine of Hippo (354–430), composed his theological works, establishing such doctrines as original sin and creating the Latin approach to the understanding of Scripture.

The popes consolidated their authority over the Western churches, and one pope, Leo I (440–461), earned the name by which is now known, Leo the Great. He did so partly by somehow convincing the dreaded Attila, king of the Huns, not to destroy Rome in 452. He also earned the title by becoming the first great papal theologian.

The fourth century had dealt with trinitarian questions; the fifth faced christological ones. How could Christ be both human and divine without the divine swallowing up the human? A theologian named Nestorius had separated the human and divine in Christ in order to shelter the human nature, but the third ecumenical council of Ephesus (431) had insisted on the unity of the two.

In 449 a theologian named Eutyches had preached that Christ had two natures before the Incarnation. After the Incarnation, the divine swallowed up the human, so that there was only one nature, a view that gained support at another council at Ephesus. Leo denounced this council as a *latrocinium*, a council of bandits, and when the fourth ecumenical council met at Chalcedon in 451, the assembled bishops, mostly Greeks, endorsed Leo's christology, which taught that Christ is one person with two natures, one human, one divine, each distinct but both united in the one person. This has been the church's christology ever since. But in Egypt the monophysite (one-nature) Christians, rejecting Chalcedon, became a powerful force and the ancestors of today's Coptic Christians.

But the empire's life ebbed away in the West, and by the end of the century the popes found themselves bishops of a proud but worn city, now ruled by barbarian Goths. Yet the church scored one more success in the West when, about 490, a British missionary named Patricius (Patrick) went to Ireland to evangelize the pagans, a task he achieved with faith and hard work, but not with shamrocks!

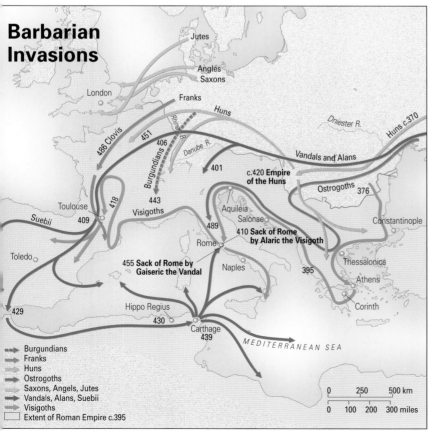

Barbarian Invasions

Jutes
Angles
Saxons
Franks
London
Huns
Rhine R.
Dniester R.
Huns c.370
486 Clovis
451
406
Danube R.
Burgundians
401
c.420 Empire of the Huns
Vandals and Alans
Ostrogoths 376
418
443
Visigoths
Aquileia
Salonae
489
Constantinople
Toulouse
Suebii 409
410 Sack of Rome by Alaric the Visigoth
Rome
Toledo
455 Sack of Rome by Gaiseric the Vandal
Naples
395
Thessalonica
Athens
429
Hippo Regius
430
Corinth
Carthage 439
MEDITERRANEAN SEA

➤ Burgundians
➤ Franks
➤ Huns
➤ Ostrogoths
➤ Saxons, Angels, Jutes
➤ Vandals, Alans, Suebii
➤ Visigoths
☐ Extent of Roman Empire c.395

0   250   500 km
0   100 200 300 miles

The Sixth Century

The sixth century saw the beginning of the separation of the churches of East and West. Barbarians ruled what had been the western part of the Roman Empire, but the Byzantine emperor in Constantinople considered those lands still under his rule. The emperor Justinian I (527–565) reconquered Italy but made it clear that he expected the popes to follow the imperial line. The popes tried to preserve their independence while working with the Byzantines, but Justinian wanted sole rule, even to the point of calling an ecumenical council (Constantinople II in 553). He kidnapped Pope Vigilius (537–555) to force him to attend. The council did good doctrinal work, but showed that the emperor viewed the church as an instrument of Byzantine policy. Yet in 568 the Lombard barbarians invaded Italy and pushed Byzantine rule back to small pockets around seaports. The West would be barbarian, not Byzantine.

Barbarian invasions caused much disruption, especially of learning, and a Roman senator named Cassiodorus (485–580) gathered monks in a monastery he had founded in Calabria, Italy, and taught them to copy books so that the treasures of the ancient world would not be lost. Later monks and nuns took up this task and quite literally saved much of ancient civilization.

The greatest figure of the age was another Italian monk. Benedict was born about 480 and died about 550. He lived briefly as a hermit, but then turned to communal monasticism, becoming the abbot of Monte Cassino. Little is known of his life, but his *Rule* for monks became the founding document for the Order of Saint Benedict (Benedictines), the monks who brought what little order there was

St. Benedict, founder of the Benedictine order.

to the chaotic barbarian world. Benedictines established monasteries throughout Western Europe, supported education, and promoted culture in the early Middle Ages and beyond.

Gregory I the Great (590–604) changed church history by turning the eyes of the papacy from East to West. He realized the barbarians were here to stay, so he worked to evangelize them, helping local bishops to evangelize the Visigoths in Spain and the Franks in France–officially Christian but with much residual paganism– and the still pagan parts of Italy. He is best known for sending a mission to England in 597 to convert the pagan Anglo-Saxons. His efforts did not always meet with success, but a corner had been turned. Western Christianity came into being.

Gregory is the traditional founder of Gregorian chant. He did not actually compose hymns, but did reform liturgical chanting.

Outside of Italy the Spanish church converted the barbarian Visigoths to Catholicism, while in Ireland the church expanded peacefully throughout the entire island.

Artist's impression of a typical medieval monastery.

The Seventh Century

The most important figure for seventh-century church history was not even a Christian. About 610 a middle-aged Arab merchant named Mohammed began to have visions that he believed to be from Allah, the only true deity. Polytheistic Arabs resisted him, but his personal magnetism and strong faith enabled him to convert the Arabs and unite the Arabian peninsula. After his death in 632, the rulers of Arabia began to expand outside their desert realm with astonishing success. The Holy Land fell to them, as did Egypt and North Africa. The homes of Jesus and his disciples, of Origen, and of Augustine, passed into Muslim hands. The Christians' world became much smaller, and now a majority of them lived in the Latin West because the lost lands had belonged to the Byzantine Empire.

The empire hosted another ecumenical council in 680–681 (Constantinople III), whose christological decrees Rome approved, but direct Byzantine influence declined in the West.

Indirect Byzantine influence, however, became significant. Many Eastern scholars fleeing Islam came to Rome, where their knowledge of Greek theology proved valuable. John IV (640–642) became the first of eleven Greek-speaking popes between 640 and 752. (They did not all reign in succession.) John firmly supported Roman traditions against the Byzantines, insisting upon the papacy's primacy and its independence from the emperor, and his successors followed that path. Greek influence became paramount; an English bishop visiting Rome wrote home that the entire papal court spoke Greek.

These popes introduced some Greek customs, for example, portraits of the saints in Roman churches took on Byzantine characteristics. They also significantly increased veneration to the Virgin Mary, made the liturgies more formal, and introduced Byzantine procedures to the papal court, putting great emphasis on the person of the pope as successor to St. Peter.

Elsewhere in the West, Ireland had become almost completely Christian, and, rather surprisingly for an island in the Atlantic, a center of Christian learning, although the greatest scholar of the day was a Spaniard, Isidore of Seville (d. 636), who wrote a widely-used encyclopedia. The conversion of the Anglo-Saxons moved along rapidly, and the French church succeeded in eliminating paganism. Much of the conversion was reinforced by the introduction of Benedictine monasteries that provided centers of learning and stability. The Dark Ages were not as dark as frequently thought.

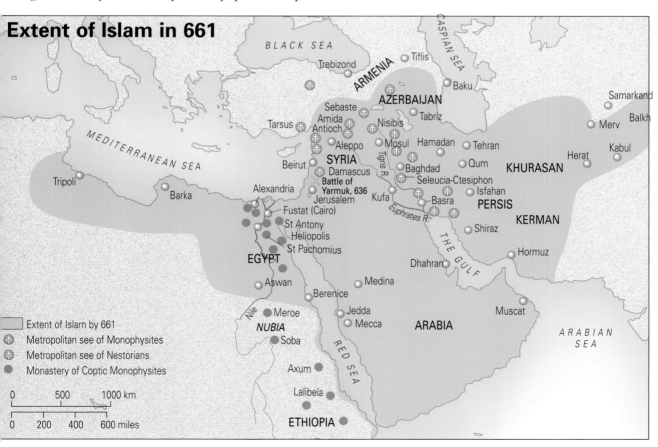

Extent of Islam in 661

- Extent of Islam by 661
- Metropolitan see of Monophysites
- Metropolitan see of Nestorians
- Monastery of Coptic Monophysites

0   500   1000 km
0   200   400   600 miles

The Eighth Century

St. Boniface, "Apostle to the Germans."

This century began with a serious loss to Western Christendom when, in 711, Arab armies conquered Spain. The population remained largely Christian, but Muslims ruled. The Arabs next advanced into France, where in 732 they suffered defeat at Tours at the hands of the Franks, a battle which saved Western Christendom. But the loss of Spain was soon offset by missionary work in the north and east as Anglo-Saxons such as Willibrord (d.739) and Boniface (d.754) converted the pagans of the Low Countries and the western part of Germany. Boniface strongly supported the papacy and spread the doctrine of papal supremacy among the new converts and among the Franks, whose support he needed.

The Franks changed the church. Their rulers, the Merovingians, had become weak and dissipated, and the family of Charles Martel, the victor at Tours, ruled from behind the throne. In 751 Charles' son, Pepin, staged a coup d'état and became king. His son Charles (768–814), a great warrior known as Charles the Great, or Charlemagne, kept up close relations with the papacy by helping defend papal lands in Italy (later called the Papal States) against depredations by the Lombards. But Charles soon made himself the Lombards' king, thus giving the popes a powerful and aggressive neighbor.

A personally pious man, Charles sought to reform the church by encouraging Benedictine monasticism, appointing effective bishops, abolishing paganism, spreading the Roman liturgy, and sponsoring a remarkable intellectual revival, which included the first serious Latin theology in three centuries. This was known as the Carolingian Renaissance.

The coronation of Charlemagne by Pope Leo III.

But Charles made it clear that he and not the pope would govern the church in the ever-growing Frankish kingdom. Since kings were sacral figures, most Franks accepted the king's role. The popes tried to restrain his ambitions, but when in 799 some Roman aristocrats created charges of misconduct against Pope Leo III (795–816), drove him from office, and tried to murder him, Charles rescued the pope. On December 23, 800, Leo formally denied all the accusations against him, and, with the king's help, regained his office. The pope had become dependant upon Charles. On December 25, Leo placed on the king's head an imperial crown, thus recreating the Western Empire, dormant since the fifth century. A new era in church-state relations had begun.

In England the Benedictine monk the Venerable Bede produced the first history of the English people, an invaluable document, while another Englishman, Alcuin, largely guided Charlemagne's intellectual revival. In Ireland monks produced the first great illuminated (illustrated) gospel books, introducing Celtic motifs into Christian art.

This century also saw another ecumenical council in the East, Nicaea II, which in 787 approved the making and veneration, but not worship, of religious images against the attacks of the iconoclasts. Rome accepted the decrees of this council.

The Ninth Century

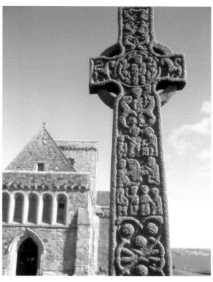

Charles was king of the Franks, but the pope had made him an emperor. Did this mean that only the pope could create an emperor? The popes thought so, but Charles' descendants contested that decision. Charles only son, Louis, succeeded him, and he gave one of his own sons the imperial title. But Louis' three sons divided the empire and fought one another for land and for the imperial title. As the century wore on, the imperial title went to the strongest, and the popes found themselves constantly embroiled in Frankish and Italian politics.

Charles' intellectual renaissance continued into this century and actually grew. A series of great scholars from all over Western Europe (Spain, Ireland, Italy, England) went to the Frankish court. Among their achievements was the creation of the handwriting (Carolingian minuscule) from which the print you are reading was derived. Also from this century are the first manuscripts of Gregorian chant that have musical notations, paving the way for the development of medieval church music. Learning also thrived outside the Frankish realm. The great Irish illuminated manuscript known as the Book of Kells was created at this time by now anonymous monks.

But this renaissance passed from history as new pagans, Scandinavians known as Vikings, began their depredations. Famous monasteries such as Iona in Scotland were attacked, and learning declined throughout the Western church. The Frankish state collapsed, local nobles rose to power, and resulting confusion crept into the church. Taking advantage of the civic disruption, Roman noble families tried, often successfully, to dominate the papacy.

Nicholas I (858–867) demonstrated that the papacy could still be a powerful moral force, for example,

by standing up for the rights of wives when noble husbands wanted divorce. He asserted papal primacy against the bishops of Constantinople, especially when Photius became bishop of the eastern capital. Nicholas considered him unworthy of the office, as did many Byzantines, and in 869–870, after the pope's death, the fourth ecumenical council of Nicaea deprived Photius of his office. But generally the Byzantines resented what they considered papal interference in their affairs. Nicholas enjoyed more success in the West, where he asserted his authority over powerful regional bishops called metropolitans. Yet one strong pope could not stem the steady decline of the late ninth century.

A Celtic cross on Iona, the Scottish island from which many missionaries set out.

Empire of Charlemagne

York
Hamburg
BRITAIN
SAXONY
Corvey
THURINGIA
Cologne
Mainz · Fulda
St Riquier · Echternach · Aachen
BOHEMIA
St Wandrille · Laon · Prum
Corbie · Rheims · Trier
Soissons · Metz · Lorsch
Rouen · Paris
Chartres · Hirsau
BRITTANY · Le Mans · Auxerre · Strasbourg · BAVARIA · Kremsmunster
Angers · Orleans · Luxeuil · Reichenau · Salzburg
Tours · Sens · St Gallen
Noirmoutier · Bourges · Besançon · ALAMANNIA · CARINTHIA
Poitiers · Ferrières
ATLANTIC · AQUITANIA · BURGUNDY
OCEAN · Limoges · Lyons · Vienne · LOMBARDY · Aquileia
Bordeaux · Tarentaise · Venice
Milan · Brescia
Embrun · Pavia
Bobbio
GASCONY · Toulouse · PROVENCE · Ravenna
Arles · Aix-en-Provence
Narbonne · Marseilles
UMAYYAD
CALIPHATE · CORSICA · Rome
Barcelona · Monte Cassino
MEDITERRANEAN SEA

	Frankish Empire at accession of Charlemagne, 768
	Conquests of Charlemagne to 814
	Marches
△	Archbishopric
⊕	Important monastery
⊕	Notable Carolingian school (and monastery)

0 · 250 · 500 km
0 · 100 · 200 · 300 miles

The Tenth Century

Canterbury Cathedral, England.

Astonishingly, the tenth century made the ninth look good. Dubbed "the Age of Iron" by historians, it saw conditions get worse as the Viking attacks on Europe were augmented by those of the Saracens, Muslims from Spain and North Africa, who plundered in Italy and southern France, and the Magyars, an Asian nomadic people who invaded East-Central Europe and who became the ancestors of the Hungarians.

The Roman nobles' domination of the papacy increased as the great families saw the papacy as a tool with which to rule the city. The nobles did not shrink from violence. Leo V (903 – 904), John X (914 – 929), and Stephen VIII (939 – 942) were murdered. Nor did they care for the dignity of the papal office; the reprehensible John XII (955 – 964) was only eighteen when his family obtained the papacy for him. The tenth century saw the papacy at its lowest ebb.

Yet God's church always has its saints. In England, Dunstan (909–988), archbishop of Canterbury, worked for both the reform of the English church and the promotion of Benedictine monasticism. His countryman Oswald (d. 992) served as bishop of York, eliminating abuses and establishing monasteries. The most important reform movement began with a French duke, William the Pious, who founded the monastery of Cluny in 910. A succession of holy and diligent abbots made Cluny a model of monastic reform. At first, other monasteries followed Cluny's lead, but soon the monastery founded daughter houses, which eventually numbered more than 1,000. Yet, successful as Cluny was, reform was also needed outside the monasteries, but that had to wait for the next century.

An important development took place in church-state relations. The German king Otto I (936–973), victor over the Magyars, asserted his supremacy over the German nobles. Otto wanted an imperial title, and it was the unworthy John XII who offered it to him in 962, so that Otto would save John from his Italian enemies. (By this time the title once held by the Frankish kings had disappeared.) Otto accepted that only the pope could crown an emperor. He marched on Rome in 962, and John crowned him emperor, thus establishing the Holy Roman Empire, which would survive until the nineteenth century. The pope quickly found that Otto thought like Charlemagne and had every intention of dominating not just the German church but the papacy as well. The political confusion of the tenth century and the distance between Rome and Germany prevented Otto from exercising too much power, but the central problem of the eleventh century had just begun.

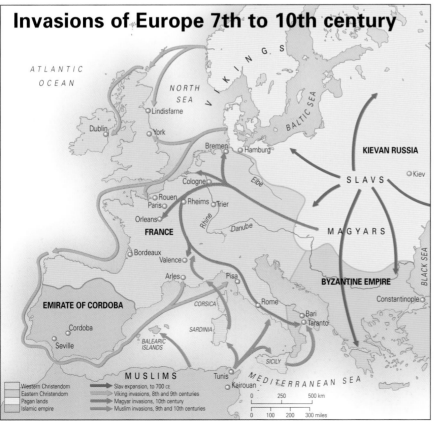

Invasions of Europe 7th to 10th century

ATLANTIC OCEAN

NORTH SEA

VIKINGS

BALTIC SEA

KIEVAN RUSSIA

Lindisfarne
Dublin
York
Bremen
Hamburg
Kiev
Cologne
Elbe
Rouen
Paris
Rheims
Trier
SLAVS
Orleans
Rhine
Danube
FRANCE
MAGYARS
Bordeaux
Valence
Arles
Pisa
BYZANTINE EMPIRE
BLACK SEA
EMIRATE OF CORDOBA
CORSICA
Rome
Constantinople
Cordoba
SARDINIA
Bari
Taranto
Seville
BALEARIC ISLANDS
SICILY
MUSLIMS
Tunis
MEDITERRANEAN SEA
Kairouan

Western Christendom	Slav expansion, to 700 CE
Eastern Christendom	Viking invasions, 8th and 9th centuries
Pagan lands	Magyar invasions, 10th century
Islamic empire	Muslim invasions, 9th and 10th centuries

0   250   500 km

0   100   200   300 miles

The Eleventh Century

When this century opened, Cluniac reform was steadily spreading and improving the religious life of the West, and leadership in the church belonged to the popes. The Holy Roman emperors dominated the papacy, appointing and deposing popes, and usually chose good men. But suppose they did not? In the middle of the century, a group of reforming popes tried to break the power of the emperor and other lay magnates over the church, and to put the papacy at the front of the reform movement. Pope Nicholas II (1059–1061) decreed that the papal voters would now be seven bishops from suburban Rome who had the honorific title of "cardinal." (The number of cardinals would increase many times over in subsequent centuries.) The cardinals first elected a pope (Alexander II) in 1061.

This renewed emphasis on papal authority strained relations with Byzantium; in 1054 the Orthodox and Catholic churches divided in a schism not healed until 1967.

In 1073 Gregory VII became pope with a determination to free the papacy from lay domination, and chose to fight on the issue of lay investiture; that is, a ceremony in which the lay lord gave a bishop the tokens of office (including vestments, hence "investiture"). Gregory said only the pope could do this. When the German emperor opposed Gregory, the pope excommunicated him, which so weakened the emperor politically that he begged — and received — the pope's forgiveness. But the emperor strengthened his hand, reasserted his control over the German church, ignored a second excommunication, and drove Gregory from Rome. In 1085 the pope died in exile in southern Italy.

All monarchs, such as William the Conqueror in England, controlled the national church, something they considered a right of office, and Gregory's view of papal authority was too exalted for this era. But his views would be taken up and furthered by his successors in the following century. Gregory had also established Rome as the unquestioned spiritual leader of the Western church. From his reign on, the papacy would play the dominant hierarchical role in Roman Catholicism.

Urban II (1088–1099), more of a diplomat than Gregory, worked with the monarchs to further reform, but he is best known for a speech he gave at the French council of Clermont in 1095, when he urged Europe's nobles to free the Holy Land from the Seljuk Turks. This triggered not just the First Crusade (1095–1099) but also the crusading movement that would last for centuries. Against almost impossible odds, the crusaders captured Jerusalem in July 1099, but Urban did not live to hear the news. The crusaders established states of their own, called *Outremer* ("over seas" in French), and introduced Latin bishops and customs, but the vast majority of the people in the Crusader States were Muslims or Orthodox Christians who loathed the crusaders.

St. Anne's church in Jerusalem, founded by the Crusaders.

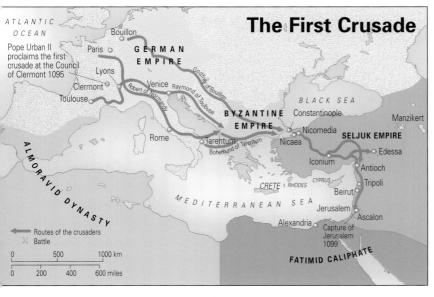

The Twelfth Century

The resurgent Muslims put great pressure on the Crusader States, and Europe mounted two crusades to help them. The Second Crusade (1148–1149) failed miserably. The Third Crusade (1189–1192) involved famous monarchs such as Richard the Lion-hearted and Frederick Barbarossa, but the Muslims kept Jerusalem and the Crusader States remained weak.

But back in Europe this was largely a century of triumph. Scholars speak of a twelfth-century Renaissance. A strong economy brought wealth to the towns, whose leaders wanted visible signs of the new prosperity in the form of large, impressive churches, known today as Gothic cathedrals. Flying buttresses made it possible to build churches ever higher and to fill their walls with the stained-glass windows that adorn cathedrals such as Chartres and Notre Dame in Paris. Ecclesiastical architecture had changed forever.

Also changing forever was intellectual life, previously dominated by monasteries. Major cathedrals founded schools to train the clergy, thus giving secular clergy educations equal to those of most monks. In 1134 the University of Paris was founded, followed soon by other universities, which now had organized curricula and awarded degrees. Soon theologians taught in the schools, and they became known as scholastics, literally "schoolmen." The greatest churchman of the century was the monastic founder and spiritual writer Bernard of Clairvaux (1090–1153), who lamented that the new learning relied more upon ancient philosophers such as Aristotle and less upon the church Fathers and monastic writers, but a new era had begun. To this day, theology is done primarily in universities.

The papacy grew stronger and more organized as papal

Chartres Cathedral, France, boasts magnificent stained glass.

government expanded to meet the popes' new role. For the first time, popes called and presided over ecumenical councils – Lateran I (1123), II (1139), and III (1179). Because the church owned much land and because the popes were temporal rulers of the Papal States, church-state problems persisted, although now both popes and monarchs normally preferred negotiation to force. But not always. In 1170 Thomas Becket, archbishop of Canterbury, paid with his life for his defiance of the English king Henry II.

Monarchs used other ways to pressure the popes. The Holy Roman emperors, especially Frederick Barbarossa, exploited political tensions in Rome to raise up antipopes whose presence always hindered papal government and sometimes raised questions of papal legitimacy, but most of Christian Europe rejected such obvious political ploys.

The four knights come to murder Archbishop Thomas Becket in Canterbury Cathedral.

14

The Thirteenth Century

St. Francis of Assisi, founder of the Order of Friars Minor.

The Crusader States remained a problem. In 1204, the Fourth Crusade attacked not the Turks but the city of Constantinople. The crusaders took it with much death and destruction, and for a half-century French nobles ruled the city. This action debased the crusading movement and caused a bitterness that still haunts Catholic-Greek Orthodox relations. Europe mounted three other crusades, but by 1291 the Muslims again ruled the Holy Land.

The growing towns of Europe had created much urban poverty and even irreligion that the secular clergy and monks could not alleviate. The Spaniard Dominic de Guzman (1172–221) founded the Order of Preachers to preach to the poor, while the Italian Francis of Assisi (1181–1226) founded the Order of Friar Minors to work with the poor. Both orders were mendicants, surviving by begging and thus identifying with the poor. As the orders grew in size and became involved in education, rigid mendicancy began to fade, but the benefit to Catholic learning was immense. The Franciscan Bonaventure (1221–1274) and the Dominican Thomas Aquinas (1225–1274) were the greatest theologians of the day, and they still influence Catholic theology.

Towns continued to build Gothic cathedrals, and both secular and ecclesiastical rulers founded new universities. Culture flourished. The earliest ecclesiastical dramas, the "Passion Plays," appeared, often in vernacular languages to explain doctrine to lay people. Gregorian chant dominated music, but composers began to experiment with new forms.

Innocent III (1198–1216), the greatest medieval pope, called the Lateran Council IV (1215), which clarified Catholic teaching on the sacraments and reformed abuses. A canon lawyer, superb organizer, and even-handed ruler, Innocent also made the papacy the political leader of Western Europe, a role his successors could not fulfill, as ambitious monarchs consolidated the first nation-states in European history and strove to free their countries from papal influence.

Political difficulties produced two unique ecumenical councils, both at the French town of Lyons (1245, 1274). The first dealt with the problems caused for the church by the Holy Roman emperor Frederick II (1194–1250). Lyons II was called by Gregory X (1271–1276), a former crusader who tried to win support for the Crusader states, a reunion with Byzantines, and an evangelization of the Mongols—none of which came to fruition.

The great basilica at Assisi, Italy, founded after the death of Francis.

The Fourteenth Century

Boniface VIII.

Boniface VIII (1294–1303) had a high vision of papal political power, but ran headlong into the modern secular state that puts its own power ahead of church teaching. King Philip IV of France wanted to diminish papal power in his country. He waged a propaganda war against Boniface, and even tried to kidnap him in 1302; the elderly pope died shortly after from the shock of this unprecedented event.

Clement V (1305–1314) was a weak-willed Frenchman, unable to stand up to Philip, who convinced the pope to go not to Rome but to the French town of Avignon, thus beginning the Avignon papacy (1305–1378). The seven French Avignon popes were good men (Urban V [1362–1370] has the title Blessed) but failed to realize that popes belonged in universal Rome, not in provincial Avignon. Also, by not being in Rome, they had to administer the Papal States at a distance, which was very expensive and contributed to the "money above all else" reputation that Avignon had.

Clement did not stand up to Philip, and the king arrested the Knights Templar, a crusading order, and took their money, proclaiming the Templars had engaged in devil worship and immorality. He also got the pope to call the ecumenical council of Vienne (1311–1312), at which the Templars were condemned.

The other Avignon popes were stronger and better, but Catholic Europe wanted the papacy back in Rome. Gregory XI returned there in 1377 and died there in 1378. The cardinals then elected an Italian archbishop as Urban VI (1378–1389). He tried to reform the aristocratic, mostly French, college of cardinals, but a group of cardinals denounced his election as fraudulent, and elected their own pope, Clement VII (1378–1394), who reigned from Avignon. The Great Western Schism had begun with the European monarchs taking sides with whichever pope they wished. In this deplorable state, the church ended the century.

But all was not bad. Important churches continued to be built, and intellectual life flourished with such scholars as the Scottish Franciscan John Duns Scotus (d. 1308) and the Englishman William of Ockham (d. 1347), best known for his theory "Ockham's razor."

When the Black Death struck Europe in 1349, the church's charitable organizations rose to the occasion. Sometimes mobs attacked the Jews, blaming them for the plague, but Clement VI (1342–1352) protected the Jews in Avignon. As always, God graced the church with saints, such as Catherine of Siena (1347–1380), famous for her work with the poor and the infirm and, significantly, for convincing Gregory XI to return the papacy to Rome.

The Great Schism

SCOTLAND
IRELAND
WALES
ENGLAND
ATLANTIC OCEAN
ENGLISH GASCONY
NAVARRE
FRANCE
Basel
Vienne
Avignon
ARAGON
PROVENCE
CORSICA
PORTUGAL
Tagus
CASTILE
BALEARIC ISLANDS
SARDINIA
ISLAMIC KINGDOM OF GRANADA
MEDITERRANEAN SEA
SICILY
Rome
PAPAL STATES
KINGDOM OF NAPLES
SWEDEN
DENMARK
TEUTONIC ORDER
LITHUANIA
Elbe
Dnieper
HOLY ROMAN EMPIRE
Danube
Constance
POLAND
MOLDAVIA
HUNGARY
Dniester
WALLACHIA
Ferrara
Bologna
Florence
Pisa
SERBIA
BULGARIA
BOSNIA
OTTOMAN EMPIRE
DUCHY OF ATHENS
ALBANIA
ACHAEA
CRETE
Loire
Seine
Rhine
Rhône
Garonne
Ebro

Roman Catholic allegiance to Avignon
Roman Catholic allegiance to Rome
Orthodox Church
Islam
Political boundary, c. 1390
Site of church council

0 250 500 km
0 100 200 300 miles

The Fifteenth Century

The schism continued to 1409, when some dissident cardinals held a council at Pisa, deposed the two existing popes, and elected a new one. But the other two did not accept the deposition, and now there were three popes. In 1414, the German Emperor Sigismund used his power and influence to get Europe's leaders to agree to a new council, held at the Swiss town of Constance. This council deposed the popes of Avignon and Pisa; the Roman pope Gregory XII (1406–1415) called the council and then resigned. Gregory's calling the council made it official. The bishops and cardinals at the council elected Martin V to end the schism but also claimed that councils had the supreme power in the church, a theory called conciliarism. (The popes never accepted this theory.) Constance also condemned for

heresy and executed the Czech reformer Jan Hus, who had a safe conduct to the council, a move that led to defections from the church in Central Europe. The council ended in 1418.

In 1431 Pope Eugene IV (1431–1447) called the Council of Basle but soon tried to adjourn it. The council cited conciliarism and continued to meet. When the Byzantine emperor tried to unite the churches to get Western help against the Turks, he contacted Eugene, who ordered the council to move to Ferrara in Italy in 1438 to meet with the Byzantines. Some members of the council moved, but others stayed in Basle and soon elected their own pope, so that there were now two councils and two popes. But the prospect of reunion won out, and Basle degenerated into confusion, although holding on until

Statue of Jan Hus, the Czech reformer.

1447 (its pope claimed his title until 1449). Eugene's council soon moved to Florence and effected a reunion with the Byzantine representatives, but when they returned home, the people rejected the reunion. In 1453 the Turks captured Constantinople, and the Byzantine Empire came to an end.

Scholars refer to the popes after Eugene as "Renaissance popes" because they had more interest in the arts than in religion, and they constantly intervened in Italian politics, often to benefit their families. Occasionally, their personal ethics fell short of what was expected of every Catholic, much less a pope. They made the Vatican a cultural capital, but the church suffered, especially as Europe's monarchs treated the popes more as politicians than churchmen. In 1492, when Columbus discovered a new hemisphere into which the church would soon expand, the notoriously immoral Rodrigo Borgia bribed his way to becoming Pope Alexander VI (1492–1503), a sad comment upon the era.

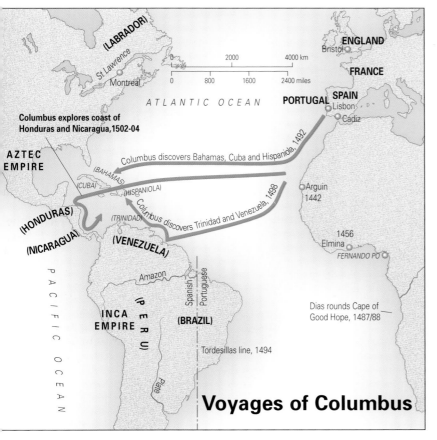

Columbus explores coast of Honduras and Nicaragua, 1502-04

Columbus discovers Bahamas, Cuba and Hispaniola, 1492

Columbus discovers Trinidad and Venezuela, 1498

Dias rounds Cape of Good Hope, 1487/88

Tordesillas line, 1494

Voyages of Columbus

The Sixteenth Century

Best known for getting Michelangelo to paint the Sistine Chapel, Julius II (1503–1513) played politics to the point of leading the papal armies in person. To fend off criticism, he called the council Lateran V (1512–1517), which his luxury-loving successor Leo X (1513–1521) guaranteed would pass good measures, but actually did nothing. When the German Augustinian monk Martin Luther challenged the basis of Catholic doctrine and insisted that only Scripture be followed, Leo's ineffectiveness allowed Luther's protest to grow into a national movement. Clement VII (1523–1534), more worried about Spanish power than the Reformation, did little to stop the spread of Protestantism in northern Europe or to find a way to keep England and Henry VIII in the church. But in 1534 a truly great pope came to the throne and began what is called the Counter Reformation.

Paul III (1534–1549) recognized that the church needed to be reformed. He appointed pious, reforming bishops to vacant sees. He gave his approval to the Society of Jesus, founded by the Spaniard Ignatius of Loyola (1491–1556). The Jesuits proved to be effective preachers, educators and missionaries who revivified much Catholic life. Most importantly, Paul called the Council of Trent, which met intermittently from 1545 to 1563. Trent clarified Catholic teaching on many issues, such as the sacraments, and passed reform decrees, such as one establishing seminaries to provide a well-educated priesthood. Trent did not reverse the Reformation, but it did commit the church irrevocably to reform.

After the council, reform devolved upon the popes, who vigorously supported it. Politics often intervened. The French kings feared that the popes' new powers would erode their dominance over the French episcopate, while Philip II of Spain (1556–1598) made it clear that he, and not the popes, would reform the Spanish church. But the popes were generally successful in imposing both reform and papal authority over most bishops, and the religious life of the church steadily improved.

The Reformation and Counter Reformation dominate the sixteenth century, but this was also a century of great expansion for the Roman Catholic Church. Missionaries spread all over the globe. Although the heroic Jesuit Francis Xavier (1506–1552) is the best known, Catholicism made little impact in East Asia, where he worked. The real gains were in the Western hemisphere, where, unfortunately, the church's work was often hindered by the ruthless imperialism of the Spanish *conquistadores* who abused, exploited, and often almost exterminated the native peoples.

Bartolomé de las Casas (1484–1566) worked as missionary priest among the native peoples from 1514 until his death. He repeatedly stood up for the rights of the natives and insisted upon their fair treatment. This angered many other Spaniards, who accused him of threatening the stability of their settlements, but, joined by other missionaries, he eventually convinced both the papacy and the Spanish monarchy to acknowledge the human rights of the native peoples.

The church's success in America was more than just a missionary one. Several dioceses were established, the most important being Mexico City, which had been founded in 1521 upon the ruins of the old Aztec capital.

The Spaniards also founded St. Augustine in Florida in 1565, the first European settlement and oldest Christian community in what is now the United States.

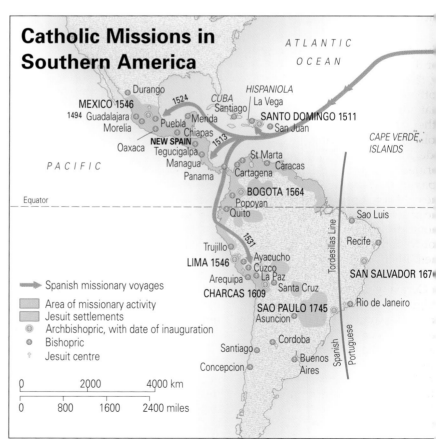

Catholic Missions in Southern America

ATLANTIC OCEAN

Durango
MEXICO 1546
1494 Guadalajara
Morelia
Puebla
Merida
Chiapas
1524
CUBA
Santiago
HISPANIOLA
La Vega
SANTO DOMINGO 1511
San Juan
CAPE VERDE ISLANDS
NEW SPAIN
Oaxaca
Tegucigalpa
Managua
Panama
St Marta
Cartagena
Caracas
1513
PACIFIC
BOGOTA 1564
Popoyan
Quito
Equator
Sao Luis
Trujillo
1531
LIMA 1546
Ayacucho
Cuzco
Arequipa
La Paz
Santa Cruz
CHARCAS 1609
Recife
Tordesillas Line
SAN SALVADOR 167
Rio de Janeiro
SAO PAULO 1745
Asuncion
Cordoba
Santiago
Buenos Aires
Concepcion
Spanish
Portuguese

Spanish missionary voyages
Area of missionary activity
Jesuit settlements
Archbishopric, with date of inauguration
Bishopric
Jesuit centre

0   2000   4000 km
0 800 1600 2400 miles

The Seventeenth Century

The baroque architecture of the cathedral in Mexico City.

This proved to be a difficult century for the popes. In the sixteenth century, the Reformation had established both Catholic and Protestant states that often struggled against each other, and this forced the popes into politics, often financing the Catholic side. Pius V (1566–1572) even formed a league with Venice and Spain to stop the Turkish threat at the battle of Lepanto in 1568. But in the seventeenth century the Catholic monarchs made it clear that they did not want the popes intervening in their affairs.

The Thirty Years War (1618–1648) in Germany demonstrated this. Originally between German Protestants and Catholics, it drew in outsiders such as Gustavus Adolphus, the Lutheran king of Sweden. The French premier, Cardinal Richelieu, feared the Catholic German emperor and thus gave financial support to the Protestant Swedes. The papacy could do nothing.

But in Italy the papacy ruled supreme. Urban VIII (1623–1644) employed the artist Bernini to add the famous *baldachino* with its twisting pillars to Saint Peter's Basilica; he also added fountains and other public sites to Rome. Yet this grandiose building scheme bankrupted the papacy. Urban also gained notoriety for the 1633 condemnation of Galileo who was teaching the new physics.

Urban's successor, Innocent X (1644–1655), opposed the treaty which ended the Thirty Years War, but the Catholic powers ignored him. He also had to deal with the most magnificent monarch of the day, the French king Louis XIV (1643–1715), who considered the church one more pawn in his absolutist approach to government. Not until the frugal Innocent XI (1676–1689) did papal finances stabilize. By then Louis XIV was espousing

Gallicanism, the notion that the French monarchy should control the French church. Innocent stood up courageously to Louis, but the French king did not change his stance.

Missions presented a brighter picture for the church. Much of South America had been evangelized, and the North American missions were expanding. The Jesuit Eusebio Kino arrived in Mexico in 1681. He soon moved on to Baja California and then to what is now Arizona, teaching the native inhabitants not only the faith but also how to live successfully in the new order the Spaniards had created. He worked in the Southwest until his death in 1711.

The French explorer Jacques Cartier had explored in North America in 1534, discovering the St. Lawrence River. But the French made no settlements until 1605, under Samuel de Champlain. Quebec, founded in 1608, became the center of New France. The Jesuits led the Canadian missions, producing several famous martyrs, such as Jean de Brébeuf and Isaac Jogues, but the missions were hampered by France's treatment of Canada as a fur-trading emporium rather than a real colony. The small settlements exercised little influence over the native peoples, who became pawns in a struggle with the English.

England had occupied the central Atlantic coast of North America with its colonies. In 1634 the first English Catholic settlement took root in Maryland, a colony founded by the nobleman Cecilius Calvert, Lord Baltimore. Surrounded by hostile Protestants, Maryland's Catholics kept a low profile, but the colony grew until 1689, when a revolution in England overthrew the Catholic king James II, deprived the Calvert family of their rights and made Maryland a crown colony.

The Eighteenth Century

In this century the Catholic monarchs continued to whittle away at the papacy's right to intervene in political matters and to assert their rule over the church in their countries. The century's best pope, Benedict XIV (1740–1758), negotiated concordats to preserve some of the church's rights and thus protect the practice of the faith. He streamlined Vatican government, strengthened seminary training, and initiated the practice of using encyclicals as teaching devices. But the monarchs were relentless. They particularly hated the Jesuits who stood up for the pope — and who had criticized the treatment of native peoples in the monarchs' colonies — and in 1773 the weak-willed Clement XIV agreed to dissolve the Society of Jesus, a dissolution that lasted until 1814. Spiritual life continued, and Benedict XIV produced an important book on canonization.

This was the era of the Enlightenment when European intellectuals established reason as the final authority in all matters, thus demoting Scripture and doctrine, unless these were deemed "reasonable." Men such as Voltaire became the forerunners of the modern secular intellectual who marginalizes religion as superstitious. Since this period, the dominant Western thinkers have been, if not outright atheists, essentially secularists (Marx, Darwin, Einstein), while religious intellectuals have been relegated by the elites to the sidelines, a blow to the church's influence but also a severe narrowing of Western intellectual life.

But Europe changed in 1789, when the long-suffering French people revolted against the royal government. The French church suffered greatly. The lower clergy were hard working and usually poor, but the bishops were all aristocrats, and many monasteries had become wealthy. Resentment toward the church led to the execution of some clergy and the flight of many more. The state confiscated and sold off church property. The revolutionary Assembly denied the pope's authority and established the Civil Constitution for the Clergy, which put the clergy under the state.

Unfortunately Pius VI (1775–1799) was an aristocrat who had spent money to beautify Rome but temporized when the French clergy needed him. He did not condemn the Civil Constitution until it was too late. He hoped that the monarchies would crush the Revolution, but in 1796 Napoleon Bonaparte brought the revolution to Italy, "liberating" part of the Papal States and occupying Rome. Fearing the now ill pope would be a focus of resistance, the French kidnapped him and brought him to France, where he died in 1799, his heroic sufferings making up for his previous hesitancy.

But while the church suffered from this revolution, another one in North America in 1776 started a new era. This century challenged North American Catholics. The British conquered French Catholic Canada, and many English colonies placed restrictions on Catholic citizens. But the American Revolution had ushered in a new form of government, one that gave preferential status to no religion but rather freedom to all of them. Freedom of religion was an Enlightenment idea, pushed by the non-religious deist Thomas Jefferson, and the Vatican and many European Catholics had grave suspicions about it. But, led by John Carroll (1735–1815), bishop of Baltimore from 1790, and a fervent adherent of the revolution, American Catholics strongly supported freedom of religion. Anti-Catholicism did not disappear, but Catholics now practiced their faith in peace and could take their place in American life. One Catholic, Charles Carroll of Maryland (the bishop's cousin), signed the Declaration of Independence, and many American Catholics sacrificed their lives in the Revolutionary War.

Charles Carroll of Maryland (left) and Bishop John Carroll (right).

The Nineteenth Century

...us VII (1800–1823) made peace ...ith Napoleon and restored the ...hurch's fortunes in France, but in ...804 Napoleon proclaimed himself ...mperor and persuaded the pope to ...ome to Paris for his coronation. ...hen Pius refused further demands, ...apoleon had him arrested (1809) ...nd brought to France, where he ...ayed until the emperor's fall. At the ...ouncil of Vienna (1815), the victori-...us nations restored the Papal States. ...ius also strengthened the church by ...storing the Society of Jesus (1814).

But the French experience made the ...opes wary of revolutionary ...ovements, even when the Catholic ...oles revolted against the Orthodox ...ussians (1832). Gregory XVI (1831–...846) so feared modern civilization ...at he would not allow railroads in ...he Papal States. Italian revolution-...ies insisted that papal government ...ust be overthrown.

Pius IX (1846–1878) had early liber-al sympathies, but when the revolu-tion reached Rome in 1848, he became the strictest conservative. Catholic monarchs advised him to democratize his government, but he refused. In 1864 he published *The Syllabus of Error*, which condemned many facets of modern civilization, including democracy and freedom of religion. Against his stern stance, the Italian revolution gained momentum, and in 1870 revolutionaries captured Rome, putting an end to the Papal States. Pius became a "Prisoner of the Vatican."

But political failure was more than matched by Pius' ascendancy in the church. In 1854, Pius proclaimed the doctrine of the Immaculate Conception, the belief that Jesus' mother Mary was born free of origi-nal sin. He later called the First Vatican Council (1869–1870), which proclaimed the doctrines of papal infallibility and the pope's immedi-ate jurisdiction in every diocese.

Yet in 1878, the cardinals chose a different kind of pope. Leo XIII (1878–1903) was a true intellectual who feared that the church would lose the new urban masses generated by the Industrial Revolution. His encyclical *Rerum Novarum* defended the rights of workers and promoted a just economic system, based on Christian values. He also attempted to improve intellectual life by a revival of Thomism, the theology of Thomas Aquinas. Although few European sec-ular intellectuals followed his lead, Thomism revivified theology and still influences much Catholic thought. Leo proved that the loss of the Papal States did not mean the loss of the pope's religious prestige.

In England John Henry Cardinal Newman (1801–1890) impressed both Catholic and Anglican scholars and lay people with his learned writings and gentlemanly manner, thus miti-gating the prevalent British anti-Catholicism.

In the United States, John Carroll became the bishop of the largest dio-cese in the world, when the lands of the Louisiana Purchase fell under his jurisdiction. He convinced the Vatican to establish new dioceses, thus allow-ing for a fuller development of the U.S. Church, especially when the bishops held national meetings. By 1860 sizeable Catholic immigration from Germany, Ireland, and Southern and Eastern Europe made Catholicism America's largest reli-gious body, which it has been ever since. Immigrants' fears of assimila-tion and the Vatican's uncertainty about America's secular stance led to the creation of a Catholic subculture of schools, societies, athletic leagues, and publishing houses. These grew rapidly and strengthened the church, but led to conservative Protestant suspicions about it. At Vatican I, American bishops defended the com-patibility of Catholicism and democ-racy, arguing that a free church pros-pered in a free state, something which many European monarchist bishops had attacked. History would prove the American bishops were right.

ineteenth-century engraving of Pope Leo XIII.

The Twentieth Century

Pius X (1903–1914) took a pastoral approach, reforming seminaries, extending communion to children, streamlining papal government, and revising the Code of Canon Law. But, unlike Leo, he mistrusted theologians who embraced modern scholarship, and the strictures he put upon them weakened Catholic theology for decades. His successor, Benedict XV (1914–1922), tried to avert World War I, but with no success. After the war, the victorious powers simply shut the pope out of their discussions, although Benedict still tried to introduce moral concerns into politics.

Pius XI (1922–1939) stood up for rights of workers, tried to establish Catholic social principles to offset the growing threat of Communism, and he emphasized the need for charity at the time of the Great Depression. His fear of Communism, however, at first prevented him from recognizing the danger of fascist governments in Italy and Germany; but, when he did see the peril, he condemned them, especially the Nazis. His efforts to prevent another war failed. In 1929 he made an arrangement with the Italian government that established Vatican City as an independent state

Pius XII (1939–1958) was a life-long diplomat who tried to prevent World War II. In the 1960s some critics called him an anti-Semite, claiming he did not denounce the Nazis harshly. As a diplomat he tried to work with governments, and feared for the millions of Catholics living in the fascist states. During the war he strove to save the Jews of Italy. After the war Pius focused on anti-Communism, especially in Europe. He promoted biblical scholarship, internationalized the College of Cardinals, and made in 1950 an infallible proclamation, the doctrine of the Virgin Mary's bodily assumption into heaven. He also became the first pope widely known via radio and television.

His successor dominates modern Catholicism. John XXIII (1958–1963) feared that the church had lost contact with the modern world. He was the first pope to address an encyclical to all people (*Pacem in Terris*, 1963), but, most importantly, he called the Second Vatican Council (1962–1965) for the purpose of *aggiornamento* or "updating." Vatican II was biblical, ecumenical, and collegial, stressing the church as the People of God, the centrality of Scripture, an openness to the modern world, the role of the college of bishops, the responsibility of the laity, the reform of the liturgy, the value of democracy and religious freedom, and the church's relation to other Christians and to those of other faiths. But John did not live past the first session.

Paul VI (1963–1978) diligently saw the council to its completion and implemented its decrees. He traveled widely, spoke at the United Nations, dialogued with the Orthodox churches, and denounced the arms race. But this good man is particularly remembered for his encyclical *Humanae Vitae* (1968), which repudiated artificial contraception. Many Catholics in democracies ignored the encyclical, creat-

John XXIII

ing a crisis of authority that continues today.

The turning point for Catholicism in the United States was the election of the Roman Catholic John F. Kennedy as president in 1960. This signified that Catholics had "made it," but it also symbolized the growing Americanization of U.S. Catholics. Many Catholics in America have moved out of urban ethnic communities and into suburbs where they interact with those of other traditions. Catholics attend college in sizeable numbers, and have moved up the social and economic scale. As educated democrats, they want their voices to be heard in the church; American bishops have not been slow to utilize lay talent, especially in parish organizations. One reason that Vatican II gave its approval to democracy was that the American church proved Catholicism and democracy can not only get along but can benefit one another.

John Paul II (1978–2005), a Pole, became the first non-Italian pope in over 400 years. A vigorous man, he traveled widely, even at risk to his life, and put the church on the side of those suffering in the Third World. He beatified and canonized more people than all his predecessors combined, and many of the new blesseds and saints are from the Third World. He helped to weaken Communism in Eastern Europe, and his many writings impacted Catholic theology.

A personally conservative man, he tried to limit what he considered the excesses of post-Vatican II Catholicism. He took a strict approach to doctrine, especially regarding marriage, women's ordination, and priestly celibacy. Many Catholics disagreed with him and Mass attendance and ordinations have declined in some regions. Yet Catholics worldwide admired this tireless laborer for human rights, and they were not alone as was proved by the crowds and foreign dignitaries who attended his funeral.

The Twenty-First Century

John Paul II, the cardinals elected Joseph Cardinal Ratzinger of Germany as the church's 265th pope, who chose to be called Benedict XVI.

...his century began with a distress-...g note. In 2002 American ...atholics learned to their shock and ...sappointment that hundreds of ...riests over several decades had ...en molesting children, and that ...me in the hierarchy had covered ... this criminal activity. Some priests were prosecuted, prominent prelates resigned their office, and the American bishops established a commission to look into the charges and to establish mechanisms to ensure that this would never happen again.

In April 2005, after the death of

...o boys stand in front of a chuch in Togoville, Tago. The chuch is making extensive ...ogress in Africa.

What is the future?
Clearly the laity will play a greater role than in the past. The priestly vocation shortage has moved lay people into occupations once reserved for clergy. Lay teachers and administrators dominate Catholic education, while parishes and even diocesan offices have a majority of lay people on their staff. These loyal Catholics are also spouses, parents, and 50 percent of them are women, so new voices from different backgrounds and with different concerns are now being heard. Understandably, some Catholics fear this change, but the hierarchy has admirably shown much confidence in these lay leaders. Vatican II called for new roles of the laity within the church, and that is happening now and will do so for decades to come.

Technology and communication mean that the secular world impacts the church as never before. Sixty percent of scientists are atheists, and since, for many modern people, science carries more weight than religion, our world will be increasingly dominated by those who care nothing for church teaching and who work in areas the church finds morally questionable, such as cloning and stem-cell research. Modern communication means that the values of Hollywood now enter our homes daily with an immense impact on children. Hollywood does not attack the church directly, but the relentless materialism and the casual, amoral sexuality on television vitiate Catholic moral teaching. This struggle can only be won on a family by family basis.

The church is rapidly expanding into the Third World, particularly Africa. African Catholics demonstrate much enthusiasm; like the earliest Christians, their faith is often charismatic and sometimes apocalyptic, a major challenge for a highly-structured, intensely

Pope Benedict XVI.

intellectual institution. The Third World churches will differ considerably from their counterparts in Europe and the Americas.

These are just some of the challenges the church faces.

As popes Gregory the Great and John XXIII proved, the church succeeds most when it keeps its essential nature but finds a way to work within the contemporary world. The church has faced many challenges before and has adapted itself to live with the good and fend off the evils of the world. The church has developed historically and will continue to do so under the guidance of the Holy Spirit. The church of the future will not be the church of the past, but it will still be Christ's church – and our church. May God bless and keep it.